W9-CLA-007

Big Science

Big Science

Nick Downes

A PUBLISHING DIVISION OF THE
AMERICAN ASSOCIATION FOR
THE ADVANCEMENT OF SCIENCE

Acknowledgment is made to the following publications, both the quick and the dead, in which these cartoons originally appeared: *Adweek's Marketing Week*, *Breakthroughs*, *Datamation*, *Enterprise Systems Journal*, *Harvard Business Review*, *The Listener*, *Management Review*, *National Enquirer*, *National Lampoon*, *Pacific Discovery*, *The Philadelphia Inquirer Magazine*, *Private Eye*, *Punch*, *The Realist*, *Research Resources Reporter*, *The Saturday Evening Post*, *Science*, and *The Spectator*.

Cartoons on pages 1 and 63, copyright © 1990 and 1991
The Saturday Evening Post. Reprinted with permission.

Library of Congress Cataloging-in-Publication Data
Downes, Nick.
   Big science: cartoons / by Nick Downes.
         p.   cm.
   ISBN 0-87168-502-7
   1. Science — Caricatures and cartoons.   2. American wit
and humor. Pictorial.
NC1429. D585A4   1992
741.5'973 — dc20   92-23435
                                                         CIP

Copyright © 1992 by AAAS Press, a publishing division of the American Association for the Advancement of Science. All rights reserved. No part of this publication may be reproduced, stored in or introduced into a retrieval system, or transmitted in any form or by any means (electronic, mechanical, photocopying, overhead projectors, slide projectors, recording or otherwise) without the prior written permission of the publisher.

Printed in the United States of America

To Annie and E.G.

You may wonder how a cartoonist expresses appreciation for the work of another cartoonist—especially one who is also a competitor for the few square inches allotted to cartoons in the few magazines that print cartoons at all. Does he laugh good naturedly? Does he slap the perpetrator on the back and congratulate him? It's more likely that he goes off into a corner and sulks. Then he mumbles to himself, "I wish I thought of that."

Can we isolate the gene that makes someone draw cartoons for a living? Nick Downes speculates in one of his cartoons that *geneticists* are forced by their genes to pursue their endless quest. Downes, unaware, is probably commenting on his own obsession. (Well, if he's not obsessed, he's at least driven.) And fortunately for all of us, the result of Downes' obsession (or drive) is a steady stream of original and topical humor, as exemplified by the drawings in this book.

You'll find in these pages a scientist who explains that he cannot put his theory into layman's terms because he doesn't *know* any layman's terms. Most people, of course, don't know anything *but* layman's terms. We can imagine (or even be acquainted with) scientists who are so immersed in their work that they are isolated from the rest of society. And the rest of society is equally isolated from the scientific world.

These cartoons serve as a two-way bridge. They provide the layman some insight into the scientific world and they allow the scientist to see the forest beyond the trees (just on the other side of the bridge). It's a bumpy ride across this bridge because it's a very funny ride.

I've often been struck by the level of detail in Nick Downes' drawings. A duck pond is not merely polluted, but has fifteen hazardous material-filled drums in it, while the pond itself is surrounded by indigenous flora. The building in the background isn't just some generic piece of architecture—it has a dormer with a picture window facing the pond.

A behavioral science lab depicts mice in two different types of cages (what other cartoonist would even think there *are* two different kinds of cages?) along with file cabinets and a maze—in addition to the people and equipment that form the subject of the cartoon. And the beakers and flasks, along with all the other trappings of daily life, are rendered by Downes in three-dimensional detail. When an artist invests so much time and energy as one of the few cartoonists paying close attention to science (you can count them on your index fingers), it's the reader who profits from the investment.

What drives Downes? It *must* be that gene.

When I see the gems in this book—and there are many, including the man with the cooling towers in his backyard and the other fellow sending out six Mother's Day bouquets—I go off into a corner, slap my forehead and mumble, "I wish *I* thought of that."

S. Harris

August 1992

"You're quite sure this goes for symbiotic relationships as well?"

"Darn it, Hawkins, when handling genetically engineered microbes, that's just the sort of thing one tries to avoid!"

"For heaven's sake, George, if it's fire they want, let them take it!"

"Let me get this straight. One bouquet goes to the mother who donated the egg. A second goes to the mother who housed the egg for insemination. A third goes to the mother who hosted the embryo and gave birth to the child. A fourth to the mother who nursed it. A fifth to the mother who raised it and a sixth to the mother who has legal custody."

"Very good, Michaels – you're a DNA molecule. Now, get back to work."

"All he thinks about is that stupid ball."

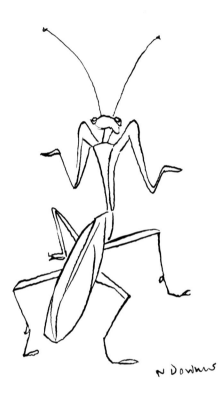

Agnostic Mantis

"I can't possibly see anyone at the moment."

"Did he say someday we'd be sorry, or Sunday we'd be sorry?"

"It's already quite apparent which is the dominant twin."

"Today's recipe for what I call 'the origin of life,' requires a bit of hydrogen, nitrogen, compounds of sulfer, carbon, a smattering of metals: iron, magnesium..."

"Mary tells me you're into phrenology."

"Heard any good anecdotal evidence lately?"

Someone other than Isaac Newton.

"It seems that only one of you is giving 100%, two are giving 80% and the rest are giving 69% or less."

"Whatever it was, it was around during the ice-age."

"Hold it, Peters — we're no longer using animals
in testing hair-care products."

"Dr. Farnsworth is attempting to isolate the gene that makes people do this sort of thing for a living."

"Salmonella."

"Eddie! — There's drift-net in the tuna-salad."

"It's our assumption, Mr. Rollins, that if one is going to make a significant contribution in physics, one tends to do so at a fairly young age."

"Try to get a little sun."

"Wake up — You're having that benzene ring dream again!"

"Throw the ball in such a way that it rotates in a forward direction, allowing the air to pass underneath the ball easier than the air above it, thereby creating pressure which will press the ball downward in a sharper arc, or curve, than would normally occur from gravitational pull alone."

"Is it user-friendly?"

"Eddie! I thought you were extinct!"

"Freud's 'Studies in Hysteria' — where the hell is it?"

1.

2.

3.

4.

NON TOXIC WASTE DUMP

NICKDOWNES

"My God, we have enough trouble competing globally."

"I didn't even know there was a union of unconcerned scientists."

"We're going to name the drug after you, Haskins. We'd like you
to change your name to miracle."

Nano-second glass.

"What was the name of that obedience school?"

"Have you any idea, young man, how much water was polluted, energy consumed, top-soil eroded, and pesticides pumped into the atmosphere in order for those beans to be on your plate?"

"Kindly take your feet off my desk."

"Would you mind stepping out of the light? I've got a solar-powered pace-maker."

"In layman's terms? I'm afraid I don't know any layman's terms."

"Yes, as a matter of fact, we are under micro-management."

"I understand the school boasts a strong science program."

"Some plants need more attention than others."

"It's something that's going around."

"Where you want 'em dumped?"

"When did you last take a vacation, Ms. Ridgeway?"

"Calm down, Helen. We've been the focus of watch-dog groups before."

"I can't help you there, Herr Doktor. I haven't the slightest idea what women want."

"The Department of Energy would like to commend you, Mr. Withers,
for refusing to take a 'not-in-my-backyard' attitude."

"Not *the* Lucy?"

THE MORE MASS AN OBJECT HAS, THE GREATER ITS FORCE OF ATTRACTION. YOU ARE EXTREMELY ATTRACTIVE.

"I can assure you, Merkins, that my mind is not under the control of space aliens, but I appreciate your concern."

"Aerobics is down the hall — this is robotics."

"Everything tastes so fresh, Mother. Where did you get the potassium benzoate?"

"The 19th? Worst century of my life."

"I think I'm beginning to grasp the concept of infinity."

"Dr. Hardwick is studying the mathematics of chaos."

"I always get it confused. Was that an example of fusion or fission?"

"Come on in — the pH is fine!"

"You're not infertile, Mrs. Simmons. Perhaps you don't breed well in captivity."

"Your great-grandmother was a pioneer in the whole aerobics thing."

"Please, Helen, I need my virtual space."

"And while we wait for the computer to call up Romans 7:8, let us open
our hymnals to number 206."

"It's a shame what happens to them under these conditions."

"It may be indistinguishable from a diamond chemically, Harry, but to me, charcoal is charcoal."

"You want a laser-scanning microscope and you still believe in Santa Claus?"

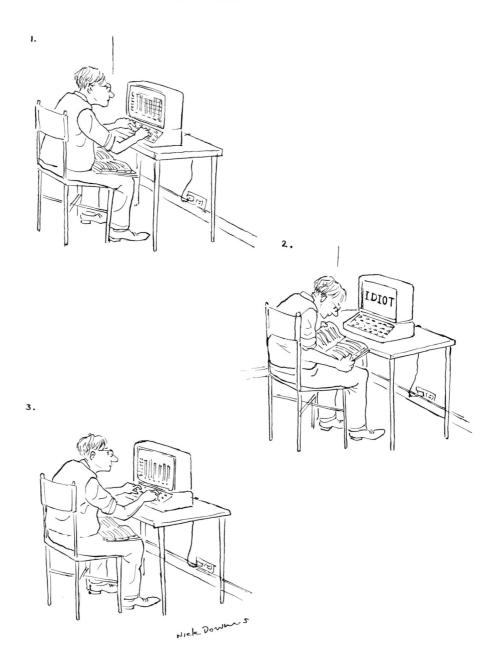

"I understand you're a high-energy physicist, Dr. Morris. Dr. Morris?"

"Gee, I dunno — those clouds look threatening."

"How 'bout now, Dugan — still want your two weeks in August?"

"Ignore him."

"Congratulations, Mr. Murtaugh, you've reached maximum entropy."

"He's nice, but he's rather obtuse."

"By God, you're right, Harris. Extremely miniature golf."

"What's worse, I'm agoraphobic."

"So far, my endorsements have been a sneaker company, a line of sportswear and the makers of a recombinant human growth hormone."

"The greenhouse certainly seems to have its effect on Hobbs."

"I don't care if it *is* a mockingbird — mocking Sinatra is going too far."

"Because it tends to trigger glands which release euphoria inducing endocrins,
I try not to smile too much."

"Surely you were aware when you accepted the position, Professor,
that it was publish or perish."

"There's something wrong with the retrieval system."

"The duck-pond could use some attention."

"Call base — tell them we may have found what's been depleting the ozone."

"Is it me or has the Pleistocene age dragged on forever?"

"Apparently big science isn't big enough for both of them."